AMBER'S DACHSHUND ANTICS

A Survival Story

Barbara Birenbaum

PEARTREE®

Published by
PEARTREE®
P.O. Box 14533
Clearwater, Florida 33766-4533 US

ISBN 9780935343816 /0935343814

Printed in the United States
10 9 8 7 6 5 4 3 2 1

Library of Congress Cataloging-in-Publication Data

Birenbaum, Barbara
  Amber's dachshund antics : a survival story
      p. cm.
   ISBN-13: 978-0-935343-81-6 (hardcover : alk. paper)
1.   Miniature dachshunds--United States--Biography. I. Title
   SF429.M52B57 2007
   636.76--dc22   2007041363

This book is dedicated to all the dogs that have been given another chance at life, and to those dogs and pets that have suffered and succumbed as a result of the tainted dog food encounter.

About the Author: Barbara Birenbaum, a naturalist, has authored three nonfiction Story Within a Story© books: *Groundhog Phil's Message,* (President's Choice - Best Juvenile Book by FPA), *Groundhog Willie's Shadow,* (in the Archives of Canada), *Amazing Bald Eaglet;* two books of quips: *Quipnotes About Moms, Quipnotes About Dads;* and eight historical fiction adventures for children: *The Gooblins' Night, Light After Light, The Lost Side of the Dreydl, Lady Liberty's Light, The Hidden Shadow, Lighthouse Christmas, Candle Talk, The Olympic Glow.* She served as poet-in-residence of Pinellas County, Florida and literature representative for the State of Florida, Division of Cultural Arts. She was author honoree at the Statue of Liberty, Groundhog Day and Olympic centennials.

Contents

INTRODUCTION

This is the incredibly true story of how one mini-Dachshund kept beating the odds of survival. Her almost eighteen years of life serves as an inspiration to those who might want to give up or give in when life throws them a curve ball.

Since this story is told in both *dog-speak* and human speak, you should know more about who I am. Dogs have played an important role in my life. Whether tall or small from Dobermans to Irish terriers to dachshunds, most have had brindle coats similar to my auburn hair. But mini-Dachshunds are more my size – petite.

I tagged along as my brother and father selected a family dog, only to come home with the one I had chosen. It may have slept on my brother's bed and met us in the schoolyard at recess, but sat through my piano practicing without howling, listened to my chatter and shared my life through the school years.

Growing up, I was the one who brought home strays and abandoned pups, only to have my mother plead, "No more pets!" However, my father nurtured my love of dogs. I was left to my own creative ways of training, disciplining and looking after them.

When our family dog got arthritis as she aged, my father and I built a cart to support her hind legs to keep her mobile. When her hearing failed, a system of hand clapping was devised. When her vision dimmed, she'd walk by my side. Dobermans created other challenges with one having its jaw realigned with wires similar to orthodontic braces and another that liked riding in cars!

Each dog had a unique personality that endeared it to our family. These beautiful four-legged friends were always considered intelligent, loving and essential to a home. Thus, when my husband and I had children, they chose an Irish terrier as their pet. When we moved to Florida and downsized our home, we also downsized to a mini-Dachshund.

The pleasure and mischief of our children's first mini-Dachshund convinced my husband and me that when and if we got another pet, it would be a mini-Dachshund. Amber's antics were enough to last a life-time. To this day my husband insists I'll probably convince him to get another brindle mini-Dachshund sooner than later.

Quips of Amber's antics offer the reader humorous tidbits, rather than dog biscuits, of how this mini-Dachshund taught us more than we could ever teach her!

FROM A DOG'S VIEW

"I made it to the patio putting my front paws down on the pool deck while easing my back legs through the sliding door. I knew to go out on the lawn, but made it as far as the sidewalk before relieving myself. And there I sat, turning my head from left to right and back again. Slowly, ever so slowly, I was taking a last look at everything in sight, even watching the birds I used to hear. Now I can only see them balancing on transmission lines between poles. Their chirping is missed!

My family patted me on the head as if I had done something good. But how could peeing on the sidewalk deserve a reward? But these were unusual times for a mini-Dachshund who was nearing her 18th birthday in October. As I looked around and up once more from my low stature on the ground, my body gave out and I rolled over on my side. This is not like me. I am frisky with a healthy heart of a much younger dog that the vet said would probably live to be 20!

That was before my encounter with tainted dog food . . .

So why are tears filling their eyes as they stand me upright? Nothing's ever that wrong that can't be righted — at least not in my mind. So I gather up my strength and walk slowly, one paw step at a time back to the sliding door, but needed help stepping over the threshold. With my body stretched out and my head resting on the riser of my dog bed I was able to watch everything that was going on.

It's a good thing, too!

9

The long and short of it is that from head to tail, though low to the ground, my responsibility to keep an eye on this family is taken in stride!

As my buddy read the newspaper on the floor, she'd stroke me occasionally blurting out a few sentences in human-speak, as if I could understand the news. I wish my feelings could be expressed in dog-speak but followed her with my eyes instead. When my family readied for the day ahead I'd usually follow them around. But today, all curled up in the dog bed, I followed them with my eyes.

It's now August 2007 and close to the end of my beginning of which I cannot recall. Then again, how many humans can remember or even imagine their beginning? It's not as easy as one thinks, especially for a dog that is long in body but supposedly shorter in memory. There are doubts about that, too!"

Thus begin the antics of Amber, the mini-Dachshund that was not always known by that name either!

THE BEGINNING

It was eighteen years ago and the end of October, an auspicious time for the birth of a brindle mini-Dachshund, one of many of a home-raised purebred litter.

"At nine weeks I was the pick of the litter by some grandchildren to bring happiness and be a companion to their arthritic grandmother. However, her living in a second floor apartment with limited ability to walk me outside was a bit beyond my understanding."

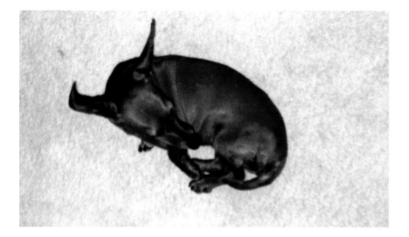

This pup, given the name Precious, came with pedigree papers, was up-to-date with shots, but was lacking a dog collar. Then again, having no contact with the outside world and being limited to an apartment-bound life style, was a collar really necessary?

"Unlike most puppies I was destined to be paper-trained to newspaper for what seemed to be forever! Most of my second chance at life was spent in a dog crate. Otherwise, I was learning what seemed to be most extraordinary antics, all things being considered in the world of dachshunds.

I barked only when the doorbell rang, waited to be fed, ate doggy treats only in the kitchen, and rarely acted out of control. However, I can only surmise this not having been around other dogs."

These later proved to be true, but that's jumping way ahead of the story. But then there were those things she was missing like a thick coat of hair and weight, essentials to becoming a healthy dog! Even by small standards a mini-Dachshund of eight months should weigh more than 5 pounds.

"Not only was I paper-trained and disciplined to stay in my crate, but became a runner, a fast one at that! The grandmother would sit or lie down on the sofa and roll a blue ball down the living room out onto the porch. I'd retrieve it at top speed and drop it at her feet or by the side of the sofa. To start another round of ball playing, I'd sit up on my haunches and drop the blue ball to the floor in front of her."

But the next paper that had any significance to this mini-Dachshund was an ad that appeared in the local newspaper under **Pet**s **-** **Dogs For Sale**. Precious was about to be given her third chance at life.

UP FOR ADOPTION

It didn't take long as a pet lover to search through the *Pets-Dogs For Sale* section of the paper to find another beloved dog. It was a hot summer day when my husband reluctantly agreed to follow up on this ad to see this 8-month-old mini-Dachshund. Together we climbed the stairs to the apartment and rang the bell. The dog that greeted us was scrawny with a thin coat of hair, but had the most talking eyes I have ever seen on a pup. She was so small for her age that if there were a breed for that size, it would have been teacup mini-Dachshund.

The grandmother explained how she was unable to care for this pet or any pet for that matter. We were told of her being paper-trained and how the only pleasure they both shared were antics with the blue ball. But there were stipulations with the purchase. Whoever got Precious must agree to take everything – the dish, the crate and the blue ball, and, above all, must promise to love her unconditionally!

There we were to possibly consider adopting Precious, while the grandmother was putting us to the test as to why an older dog was preferred. Her concerns were put to rest when told that a more mature dog - one that had been trained - would make an easier transition for both the dog and us as her new owners. We left to think about our preference for this mini-Dachshund, or any dog for that matter, at this stage of our lives when children were in college, giving us time to have more privacy and spend time together.

"Instinctively, I knew that my tail wagging and facial expressions as a dog could let them know how I felt. But as they looked at me I let my eyes do the talking, hoping beyond hopes that I would be theirs!"

In our heart-to-heart discussion at lunch, two separate conclusions were reached. My husband insisted there was no way this particular dog would be part of our lives! Especially after rebounding from the loss of another mini-Dachshund.

Thinking about the talking eyes standing out against her scrawny body, this loved but no-longer-wanted pup needed another chance to enjoy her life! In my heart I knew we could give her a loving home.

Our discussion went back and forth. Just as it seemed to be going more backward than forward, the car headed toward the apartment for one more look. The look turned into love. We left with the dish, the ball and Precious in the crate. From her birth in a litter of pups to being loved and cared for by a grandmother, she was about to get a new family!

From head to tail, this dachshund came with enough antics that stretched longer than her body, if such things could ever be measured. And they kept emerging as she grew.

A NEW BEGINNING

"I neither whimpered nor barked when taken from my environment and security to a new home. How could I when I don't really know what to expect! Better to take everything in and enjoy this new adventure and car ride for now."

The more that is told about this pup, the easier it is to understand her special gift of talking with her eyes, though we remained amazed when she never whimpered.

"This was only my first ride of many that takes an entire lifetime to experience. The next ride is in a four-wheeled shopping cart. For the likes of me I don't understand the importance of getting a dog collar. But that also plays an important role in my life. For now I'll just enjoy the trials of a new beginning."

The first stop to purchase a small collar and name tag to go with the vaccination tag presented a challenge. A cat collar seemed the best size-wise, but they were too gaudy. Finally after trying on collar after collar and searching for one other than blue, a red one was found that wouldn't slip off over her head.

And then there was the question of her name. Precious???

The name was befitting a beloved darling pup, but neither of us felt it was a real name for a frisky dog. So, this brindle mini-Dachshund began her third chance at life with the name Amber, more suitable for a dog whose personality was about to add color to our lives!

"In dog-speak, though I no longer hear the name Precious, I am sure to get a quick response when called by the name Amber.

Once home, the crate was put in the family room, the dish in the kitchen and the collar with tags was placed around my neck. What a weird sensation when the coldness of the tile floor was sensed through the pads of my paws. Like any other mini-Dachshund or dog, it was time to explore the new surroundings."

We watched as she walked around with the tags jangling almost as low as she was to the ground. But never suspected anything unusual  would happen, even as she started to explore from inside to outdoors – a place she had never been before.

Her first encounter with the outside world came shortly thereafter. She walked down the hall, through the family room, out the kitchen sliding door, and scampered across the pool deck. Stopped! Walked around the edge of the pool as if to size up the situation. Stopped several times to peer in. Then took a dog-dive paws first into the water! Her long body resembled a canoe as she tried to paddle her way to safety!

With dog tags and collar weighing her down like an anchor, she sank! But this pint-sized pup was retrieved quickly! After gasping and gagging, with every breath of fresh air she inhaled the little water she swallowed was expelled! We were happy and relieved that she had survived this new experience. This auspicious antic was only another beginning to her also becoming a swimmer!

"I may have been taken aback by what happened, but this was no time to whimper. After all, I'm the nosy pup that jumped in and dog paddled before going under only to be saved.

I had to stay alive! There's no way I'd be a goner with so many new things to explore. With forelegs outstretched I bounded into the tall grass eager to run!.

But found myself hopping and jumping like a jack rabbit when it tickled my underbelly. It was time to move on and nose around the house."

After this experience, Amber walked up to, looked over, but rarely stepped down into the sunken living and dining room unless she slipped and slid across the tile floor into the rooms running after her ball.

For all we know, the edge of the walkway around the rooms could have reminded her to watch where she stepped or else sink as she did in the pool.

At this young age, Amber seemed to be making associations, transferring memory from one experience to help her through the next. This would serve her well in years to come.

Amber kept her nose out of trouble until she decided to unearth her way out of the yard through a fence that was beginning to show its age.

"It didn't take much digging to get under the back yard fence. It was even easier to squiggle under some boards into the neighbor's yard, or from one neighbor's yard to the next. Sometimes being small was a plus, especially when I could nose my way through small openings just to nose around!"

This nosy pup gave up this antic only after being unable to retrace her route or dig her way back into the yard.

Amber seemed to know that if people went through a fence gate, she should too! So if we were in the front yard and she was out back, the sidewalk we thought would be a deterrent didn't keep her from digging under or around it to get through the gate!

 The pothole she dug between the sidewalk and fence post forced us to put a patio block between the two. Even then she was determined to nose her way out. At first she'd

just peek under. Then she'd nose a bit further, until finally nosing her entire head under the gate, oftentimes getting it caught.

"There's no way this fence would keep me in if I really wanted to get *out! I don't know how* *else to tell them it needs* *replaced except by dig-* *ging or nosing under it."*

This new nosy antic continued until her message in dog-speak convinced us that our home definitely needed a new fence. Not just any fence, but one with a pressure-treated baseboard, often called a pet board, to keep her in the yard when she was outside.

CURIOSITY PUP

She had already encountered four chances at life and survived each as if nothing had happened! Once her footing was secure in her surroundings, she was on the go outside chasing snakes, squirrels and salamanders while eyeing the chirping birds.

Amber chased ducks, snakebirds and other dogs right to the perimeter of our property line. Another something she sensed that seemed unexplainable!

However, she'd bark at box turtles that had free reign of our enclosed garden, and became a nuisance nosing and rolling them over. We could never figure out whether she thought they were balls to play with or her dachshund instinct was to bury them in the mulch.

"With digging deeply rooted in my dachshund nature, it was instinctive to bury anything I sensed should be buried including turtles. However, they snapped back or clammed shut unlike bones and other treasures that got buried outside!"

And as fast as her memory was logging in experiences for future recall, she was finally growing – slower than faster and staying low to the ground! Her ears flapped as she scampered, and her tail wagged more often to the right than left - supposedly indicating more pleasure. If these were communication skills, we were about to learn more dog-speak . . .

Amber pointed at the pantry door for

food and treats. She could have gone out any door to relieve herself, but always pointed to the kitchen slider to go out back. She walked alongside my husband without a leash. When she explored scents in the grass, he'd call and she'd return to his side.

"Being long in body and even longer in stride I stretched the limits of behaving by wandering off, but not so far off that I wouldn't hear the word 'Come!' In all honesty, running when called kept me on the move and in some ways refined my athletic abilities so natural to dachshunds."

If dogs played baseball, Amber became a champ!

Endless hours each day were spent with one of us throwing the blue ball down the hall, in the kitchen, from the family room down another hall. Blue marks on wood trim and walls were reminders of her ball-catching efforts. Good thing there was an extra supply of interior paint, for the brush was always painting something.

Later, the blue ball became an indicator of her well being!

If we went outside, she'd follow. My pitching arm developed as she ran faster and farther to retrieve the ball from the yard. And when sweat got the better of us, we'd all go in the pool.

Let's put that in perspective. She'd bark at us and run around the pool wanting to come in, until she was put in the deep end and swim to the shallow end. With hind legs holding her upright on the step and front paws on the deck, she'd wait to be lifted out. The chlorine may have killed the fleas, but the shampooing after each swim gave her coat a healthy sheen.

Amber may have been small for her age reaching all of nine pounds, but tall in stature, especially when she visited the kennel, better known as kennel college. Her tail wagged as she went in and took her position as "leader of the pack" whenever the dogs went outside.

"I may be a family dog, but that strong

hunter instinct to lead I've inherited as a dachshund took over when con- fronted with a group of dogs no matter what their size or breed."

Being powerfully energetic, she often enjoyed playing ball down the halls of the kennel. If the vet techs got sore arm from throwing, she was the reason why! No wonder they were happy to see this bundle of energy come and eager to have her return home, only to continue her blue ball antics.

When our college kids returned for visits, at first they'd be ignored. But whoever played ball became instant friends!

Over the years, if she heard the garage door opening and suitcases being rolled into the bedrooms, Amber would park herself with her blue ball in their rooms until being relocated to her own bed! She watched with a mournful look when they left, and would mope around in their rooms for a day or two hoping beyond hopes that they'd return sooner than later.

THINGS HAPPEN IN THREES

Amber, now eight years old, had trained the family to her routine. She rested and played by our schedules but had her own sense of timing! Daylight Savings Time may come and go, but she always wanted food at the same time each morning – seven o'clock sharp! Then, after a snooze, she'd be out and about, playing ball and chasing everything in sight in the yard.

That was fine until the day the soil around the property got treated for termites. Unbeknown to us, this chemical was absorbed through pads of her paws causing her to be quite ill. So ill, that we thought she was a goner.

But not Amber! This dog had already been given many chances at life. How toxic could termite poisoning be? But her reaction to this incident seemed different! Concerned about its effect we were headed to the vet when the airbag in the car imploded.

Amber was sent flying over the front seat only to land on all fours in the back seat. Soaring through the air she may have been traumatized, but never even whimpered in pain or shock! When a jogger passing by opened the rear car door to take her, Amber jumped to the street. But she outran the jogger who tried to catch her as she made a dash up the road to a major highway.

But Amber's running was no match for

the zooming cars that hit her!

What started as a dash for survival turned into a major retrieval of our mini-Dachshund. Thanks to the name tag, a policeman who rescued her brought her to our home. Since we weren't home, he took her to our neighbor. They, in turn, took her to the local Veterinary Emergency Clinic.

"Luck was with me when the name tag purchased so many years ago enabled the policeman and clinic to contact my family. They may think I'm a goner, but I know I'm going home!"

If Amber even thought about her determination to live after the termite poisoning, she was about to be confronted with another challenge! After spending the night in Critical Care of the Emergency Room, the next day's diagnosis for survival wasn't encouraging.

Since she hadn't relieved herself for a day and also had lacerations, broken bones and possible paralysis from the waist down, we were advised to put her to sleep.

Tears welled up in our eyes seeing her faced with another trauma. Once more, she was put in her bed in the kitchen as we decided how to handle the medical advice. But then Amber did something quite extraordinary.

She dragged her injured body into the family room placing her head, upper torso, and forelegs on the rug. Then she relieved herself, on the tile floor from the family room all the way into the kitchen!

Who says this dog is a goner??? Not our Amber. In our hearts this was a sure sign that she would live, and this was the only way she could let us know.

Again, not so much as a whimper was heard!

This time she was taken to our vet who had already watched her survival rate go beyond the normal span. No matter what happened, we were becoming accustomed to his usual phrase, "Let me run some tests." This vet always anticipated the positive outcome to situations. As Amber matured, this would make a great difference in her staying alive.

But for now, Amber spent the next week in the veterinary hospital on intravenous, hydration and medications that also flushed out the termite poisoning. Lacerations were on the mend. However, with possible paralysis, the broken pelvis and injured hind leg were left to heal on their own if they could!

Again the diagnosis after the first week of recovery wasn't good. We were again faced with the decision of putting Amber to sleep. After coming home, she was carried around the neighborhood in our arms to say good-by to the birds, salamanders and other dogs.

They didn't know it was her final good-by.

And soon it became apparent that she didn't know or accept it either.

Once more she was put in her bed in the kitchen as we pondered her fate. While we rested on our bed in decision-mode from mounting tension, in came Amber using her forelegs to drag herself from the kitchen, down the hall to the bedroom with the blue ball in her mouth. When it was dropped by the bed, she gave a loud *"woof"* as if to say *"Ball playing time!"*

We knew she had to be in pain, but not a whimper was heard! In her own way she was sending us a message with the blue ball.

"If I can play ball, I will live!"

That blue ball was becoming a barometer of her well being!

With tears of hopefulness in our eyes we again sensed that Amber would be a survivor.

35

Encouraging news came from my cousin, a veterinarian at the Animal Medical Center of New York City, to have someone rotate her back legs in water as often as possible. A groomer volunteered her services.

Since Amber was eating, sleeping and relieving herself, there was a good chance that the pelvic bone and whatever other small fractures she had would heal. That was March of her eighth year.

By June she and I were going in the pool together. She had become a three-legged swimmer, until the right hind leg was forced to rotate with hydrotherapy in the water! Soon, the leg became sensitive to touch – a sign that feeling was returning!

Through all of these months of what had to be pain, Amber never whimpered.

By July, Amber was walking on all fours, but ran on three at times. By August the 12th to be exact, she stood on her back haunches, dropped the blue ball at our feet and *"woofed"* for us to play ball!

Amber was the comeback mini-Dachshund that had now survived three more chances at life. She had an inner strength and determination to live! If she was experiencing pain, she never let us know. Never put it past this dachshund to show us with her antics that she was on the mend.

LET'S PLAY DOG-BALL!

Three months of hydrotherapy in a large tub and two months of swimming pool therapy, Amber was back to normal – as normal as a dog could be with a crook in her right hind leg and a hump in that pelvic area. But her eyes said it all . . .

"Here I am! I'm myself again! I can stand - I mean truly stand! There's no way I'm a goner! Of course, I always knew I'd make it. The vet knew I'd make it. The vet techs knew I'd make it and my family believed in me!"

Amber seemed to know that the secret to overcoming adversity was to confront it. And to overcome pain, give no hint of discomfort – In this case, not even a whimper!

And with more life ahead of her than behind, she was ready to take off – from her bed, to running around the house and out through the garage door.

"Here I come world!"

Out scampered Amber down the drive-way, across the yard, down the walk and around the cul-de-sac. Lacerations healed and were hidden by hair. But the hind leg and hip were a bit off-kilter.

That didn't stop Amber from running her usual path. Although as a fast runner, she lifted her right leg to let three do the work of four. Once back in her normal stride, she became the four-legged mini-Dachshund run-ner!

And, she created her own sport – a dog-ball game of endless innings or outings dependent on whether it was played indoors or outside. We'd forever pitch and she'd forev-er catch the blue ball that had been with her forever! Amber zoomed to retrieve it.

Dog-ball was not the pastime of a few

throws a day, but became more of a full-time, daily event. This ball playing occurred everywhere at any time, whenever we were watching TV and whenever she thought we needed something to do!

As with all things, eventually the blue ball got lost only to have Amber bark for its retrieval.

Our arms got some relief when it landing out-of-sight behind the TV console, or in both real and artificial plants hiding like camouflage in the leaves. The longest time without the ball was two weeks when it landed in a shoe that got closeted, once retrieved only to disappear again.

One week went by and still no blue ball!

She was like a child without a security blanket – no other ball would do! Several were purchased with bumps, scents and bells, but all were totally ignored!

"Of course these balls were ignored! The bumpy ones are too bumpy for my small mouth. Why would I want to hear a bell in a ball when I can see it bounce? And I'd much prefer a scented bone to a scented ball that can't be chewed! I know where that smooth, blue racket ball is if they'd only listen!"

Amber barked at the planter until it and everything close by was moved. The following week, after putting up with the talking eyes and nose that kept sniffing around the planter, the basket inside was removed. Beneath it was the blue ball! How it got there we'll never know. But her keen sense of smell helped solve the dilemma.

Amber had more living to do! That meant more ball playing and exercise. Sitting on her haunches, the blue ball would be dropped to signal the start of a ball game. She also continued chasing birds and salamanders and running around the cul-de-sac daily.

But one house from the corner where the zooming sound of whizzing cars could be sensed on the county road, she would stop running abruptly! Perk her head. Listen to the noise of cars. Cross the street, turn around and head for home. The noise alone probably reminded her of the encounter with cars.

If this mini-Dachshund is living proof, dogs definitely have a memory and good recall!

A MIND OF HER OWN

Amber was enjoying her maturity and claimed new territory – beds in the family room and office to keep an eye on us while we worked, and her own rug in the master bath.

Added to her ball playing, swimming and napping routines she continued to enjoy the kennel as leader of the pack to go outside. She enjoyed chasing the ball down the kennel corridor and seemed to have free reign to run! She wagged her tail to go and seemed to enjoy each stay!

"Wish my family could understand dog-speak to take more vacations so I can have fun on my own vacation at kennel college or kennel camp dependent on the season. Maybe they'd like an early kennel wake-up at home."

Close to 7 o'clock every morning, Amber became an alarm clock tugging at my side of the blanket to get up and let her out. She looked at food and fresh water put in her dish as if to give her nod of approval. Then curled back up in her bed for a mid-morning nap, saving eating for later.

Other times she tussled with her rug in the bathroom, folding it over and dragging it atop a larger bath rug until it was contoured into a bed for snoozing. Once she snuggled into this bundled heap for a nap, there was no moving her or the rug without a look of disapproval and repositioning the heap.

"Wonder if they realize how much pawing and nudging it takes to tug and pull a rug much larger than me into a cozy bed. After all that effort, surely they can just step over me whenever I'm resting!"

And we found ourselves doing just that!

Amber had a mind of her own. My husband often wondered why new rugs to match the bathroom décor were stored in the closet.

Better to be prepared to replace rugs "under destruction" than replace an entire master bath décor.

How wonderful that we are awakened so she can go back to sleep! We can only surmise that she slept at night with one eye open to protect us, as if she needed an excuse for an extra daytime snooze.

Evening became a totally different routine, as her nose pointed to the door around 6 o'clock waiting for her buddy, my husband, to return from work. Any urge to go out was suppressed until his arrival. But that was only the beginning.

She'd wait for us to finish dinner, and then look at us with those talking eyes for tid-bits, but preferred fish. We wondered if she was part cat. The vet insisted the Omega-3 fish oil she consumed plus her ball playing and running kept her heart healthy and her body trim! We tend to agree.

After dinner Amber and my husband would take out the garbage together. He'd hike and she'd run around the cul-de-sac, stopping one house from the corner, turn around, cross the street and run the cul-de-sac in reverse.

But that was only the beginning of her evening antics!

Afterwards, she would dash into the kitchen and point to the pantry door for treats. It's not that they were needed, so much as deserving a reward for taking my husband on a walk! If ignored, she'd follow him and *"woof."* Or, better still, she'd just *"woof"* at the pantry door until he gave in.

Amber was one determined dachshund!

Her evening antics continued when she'd curl up on his lap for a rest. And at 10 o'clock or thereabouts, since we wondered if she counted the chimes of the clock, she would lead him to the sliding door to go out.

One dog with a mind of her own divided her quality time between us as if she was doing each of us a favor.

If I was left alone with her in the evening she wasn't as cooperative, often needing picked up and carried to the grass! Likewise, my husband never ever got a blanket wake-up tug in the morning.

KEEPING UP WITH AMBER

The years zoomed by and Amber's antics continued as if she was much younger than her fourteenth, fifteenth, and sixteenth years!

Though she was used to adults, not having been raised around children had its drawbacks. Especially when one very special little girl loved Amber as the pet she always hoped to have. Initially, whenever the girl ran up to her, Amber would run the other way but never snarled or growled!

She was as eager to learn how to pet Amber as she was determined to have this dog, that was more her size, as a friend! Soon they'd look for each other! She'd call to Amber when they were outside. She also ran outside to play whenever Amber stopped at her driveway looking for her during runs around the neighborhood.

These evening visits with tail-wagging Amber were especially enjoyed when they played together past her bedtime!

Other times the little girl would come by the house, look up and ask hoping beyond hopes, "Can Amber come out?" They'd talk and play and their friendship grew.

"It's only natural that with my more placid personality surrounded by adults I'd prefer being left in peace. But like playing ball, I am always learning! By enjoying my new buddy, I also became more comfortable around others."

New pet items came on the market as pet ownership became the rage. The dental breath-cleaning dog bone sounded great! One was purchased! Amber wagged her tail, took it outside and buried it! We assumed she was chewing on it outside in-between ball playing and chasing salamanders.

Several bones later that all ended up buried we came to the conclusion that the manufacturer was dog savvy, making a fortune selling an item that never got used for its intended purpose. This dental cleaning bone required more purchases to replenish the supply of those that vanished – lining the pockets of the creator with money.

As she grew older, the vet pronounced Amber healthy with a heart of a much younger dog. So much younger that we all anticipated she would live to be twenty, a very old age for a mini-Dachshund.

"My only telltale signs of aging were paws and whiskers that turned gray. I'd swim in the pool several times a month and enjoyed my status as the elder dog of the neighborhood and kennel.

Even as my hearing diminished I not only responded to everything with my usual energy and pep, but to hand clapping unless deep voice commands were heard. As my visual acuity sharpened, the birds that could no longer be heard were watched. And I continued chasing squirrels and salamanders and running after my blue ball."

Amber continued to point for attention or when she wanted something, whether it was to the pantry, the sliding back door or garage door to go out. Oftentimes, we were at a loss understanding this mode of dog-speak. Especially when she'd point from one room, assuming we understood that what she wanted was in another.

Her acute vision compensated for her limited hearing. Around people she would often stop in her tracks, turn her head to observe what was going on around her, then react with her talking eyes, a wagging tail, or by running or sitting.

If approached unexpectedly or touched from behind, she'd jump. So the young girl would come face-to-face with Amber. Then she was shown how to gently touch the dog's nose to give Amber a "scent of security" before petting her! She also clapped to get her attention, quickly adapting to Amber's new modes of communicating by seeing, sensing and pointing.

However, Amber seemed to be more protective of grandchildren who could tussle and even include her in their play! But even with them she'd often stop abruptly, turn her head, and pause before continuing with her antics or participating in their fun.

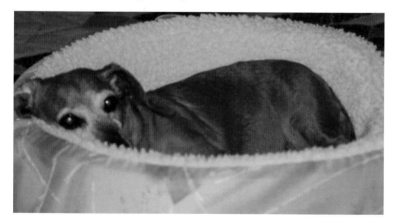

TAINTED DOG FOOD

Amber was beyond her October birthday, and romped through the holidays. But with the New Year 2007 strange things happened. She drank what seemed to be buckets of water, had to relieve herself many times throughout the night leaving occasional puddles on the floor and started losing weight. She looked forward to fish tidbits, but then walked away. She'd walk outside but no longer zoomed. And then there was the blue ball she'd watch as it rolled down the hall but wouldn't retrieve. Other times it was with her in her bed.

Remember, this blue ball was the barometer of her health!

Thinking she was a goner, she was taken to the vet Friday, February 9th to be put to sleep. But the vet, who believed in Amber's well being came up with his usual phrase,

"Let me run a few tests." The report confirmed renal failure. But we were assured that with such a healthy heart, she would survive!

After another week in the hospital, she returned home on medicines and a regimen of kidney, K/D, dog food. How could such a healthy dog become sick so quickly?

That was just before news of the tainted dog food . . .

The recall of tainted dog food from China, distributed by Menu Foods of Canada, made news Friday, Feb. 16th for possibly causing kidney failure in both cats and dogs. The pouch food fed to Amber was on the list.

That explains how an otherwise healthy dog suddenly suffered renal failure. Likewise our vet was dog savvy enough to know, at least with our dog, that she would live!

Through all of this Amber never even whimpered!

"RECALL has pet owners worried"

"Pet owners wonder if food affected their pets"

the Humane Society of North Pinellas.

One worker on Saturday went to a Web site to research the suspect brands and lot numbers, while others removed a relatively small number of cans or packets off the shelves.

The news left many wondering about troubles that recently befell their pets.

In Clearwater, author Barbara Birenbaum said her 17-year-old mini Dachshund Amber got so sick in February with kidney disease and dehydration that she was afraid the dog would die.

Her veterinarian put Amber on a special kidney diet 'and she slowly recovered.

St. Petersburg Times, Tuesday March 20, 2007. "Recall has pet owners worried"

Each day on the medicine and K/D dog food she seemed to be on the road to recovery. But the medical follow-ups continued to show renal failure. The damage had been done, but hopefully not too much for her to regain her pep, energy and ball playing antics!

Amber was rewarded with a savory scented peanut butter bone for being on the road to recovery. We should have known better. The dog savvy manufacturers duped us again when she buried it outside! Dachshunds are true diggers, for it has yet to be found!

No more scented bones for Amber!

She had become the comeback dog always beating the odds of survival. Even with a strong heart, slowly, ever so slowly Amber's life took a turn for the worse. She tried to play ball and chase salamanders. She tried to take long walks and would occasionally zoom a few houses around the neighborhood as if to say, *"Look at me. I am a survivor. I can still run. Watch me!"*

But we found ourselves watching her and watching out for her!

It was the end of July. Amber followed us with her eyes everywhere. She skipped meals. She watched my husband as he took out the garbage with the talking eyes that said, *"I'd like to get up and go with you but can't. Not today!"*

An appointment was made with the vet for another evaluation the afternoon of August 2nd. But whatever was wrong couldn't wait until then to be diagnosed.

By the time she arrived at the clinic that morning in her bed with her blue ball we thought she was a goner. Tears welled up in the vet tech's eyes and they poured down our cheeks. As I petted Amber there was still a heartbeat. The vet came in and confirmed that indeed her heart was still beating.

"They thought I was a goner, but I'm a mini-Dachshund!"

Again he left. Again we thought she was gone. Again the vet returned to find her heart beating ever so slowly. We knew she was trying to make a comeback. We also knew that her time had come.

With her body ravaged by whatever happened as a result of the renal failure, there was only one option at this point.

Amber went to heaven as tears welled up in our eyes again. No matter how much she suffered, her determination to live won out. And she never whined with pain, even when it became apparent the tainted dog food did her in and accelerated her demise.

She was a beloved mini-Dachshund whose blue ball antics became a messenger of her well-being. Her heart will forever beat in the lives she has touched. She didn't ask anything of life but to be given a chance and she was given eight chances that spanned almost 100 years in dog life.

There is a bit of Amber in us, and all living things, to overcome adversity with the will to survive.

Sometimes the talking eyes of a loving pet show more emotion than could be expressed with a whimper or woof.

And the blue ball is a reminder that each pet has its own barometer in the ballpark of living.

ORIGINAL QUIPS
AMBER'S DACHSHUND ANTICS

Dogs rest when people are on the go.
Dogs are on the go keeping people from resting.

Dogs are for pet lovers.
Dogs love to be petted.

Dogs have antics all their own.
Dogs color people's lives with their antics.

Dogs learn to come on command.
Dogs command attention for what they've learned.

Dogs go in circles before settling down.
Dogs settle down in a circle on your lap.

Dogs play ball for exercise.
Dogs think people need exercise, so play ball.

Dogs stride along side people.
Dogs take protecting people in stride.

Dogs that are active tend to be healthy.
Dogs enhance the health of people by their activity.

More about dogs . . .

Dogs figure out how to behave without knowing math.

Dogs give ground only if they're barking up the wrong tree.

Dogs that bark up the wrong tree may need a ladder.

Dogs give-and-take whatever they can take without giving up!

Dogs are complex, making heads and tails of situations at the same time.

Dogs that are hard of hearing use other senses to react.

Dogs often find a ball the barometer of their health.

Dogs that play ball are usually good sports.

Dogs think people know few words repeating them over and over.

Dogs have a depth of understanding we have yet to understand.

On the go . . .

Dog days may find the dog in the swimming pool.

Dogs let go of balls only if they are thrown again.

Dog's lives may be touch-and-go when they should be get-up-and-go.

Dogs are always on the go, even when age slows them down.

Dogs that go to bat for people often play ball!

Dogs seem to know . . .

Dogs wet nose nudges let you know they're around.

Dogs have one sense of direction – forward.

Dogs have the ability to understand commands in different languages.

Dogs take people at face value with no money attached.

Dogs light up your life without a flashlight.

Dogs are good friends that never let you down.

DEVOTED DOG ©
By Barbara Birenbaum

In this *dog-eat-dog* world
of human existence
where *dogs are people's best friends*,
we share your emotional loss.
In the *dog days* of recalling
your favorite pet's
many mischievous adventures,
know that your pet who
was never too *dogtired*
to protect you on earth,
stands as a *watchdog* from heaven!
Memories of this *pawful* good friend
will last a lifetime.

This poem is dedicated to those pets that have
gone to their final resting place.

LOSING A *pet* IS LOSING A *good friend.*

Amber was such a sweet girl. She will be greatly missed. *Kathy*

We all loved Amber, we will miss her so much. We'll keep her in our prayers. *Dean S.*

So Sorry *Lyn*

The first time I saw our Amber, she stole my heart.... I loved her too!! She earned her wings and enlightened all of our lives *Lynn Wolf*

Hope time will help to ease your sorrow.

VERY sorry for your Loss *Terri Manders on*

It's so very difficult to lose such a great friend. *Pamela*

Reproduced by Permission American Greetings Corporation ©AGC. Inc.